Master Evernote

Organize Your Life and Get Your Crap Done Using Evernote!

The Comprehensive Masters Guide to Evernote

Table of Contents

Introduction 3

Chapter 1: Evernote – General
Information 7

Chapter 2: Evernote – Free versus
Premium 15

Chapter 3: The Evernote Desktop
Application 21

Chapter 4: Evernote – Smartphone
Applications 24

Chapter 5: Tips and Tricks 33

Chapter 6: Evernote Plugins and
Add-ons.. 52

Conclusion 55

Introduction

I want to thank you and congratulate you for downloading the book, *"Master Evernote: Organize Your Life and Get Your Crap Done Using Evernote!"*

This book contains proven steps and strategies on how to master the Evernote service.

This eBook will explain the basics of Evernote. By reading this learning material, you will know important things about the desktop and smartphone applications of Evernote. You will also learn how to create excellent notes and to-do lists using different devices. Finally, you will get great tips and tricks that can help you maximize the benefits you can enjoy from this valuable computer software.

Thanks again for downloading this book, I hope you enjoy it!

Chapter 1: Evernote – General Information

Evernote is an application designed to help people create, organize and archive notes. It is a cross-platform application. You can use it with different types of gadgets (e.g. smartphones, tablets, laptops, etc.). In addition, it is classified as a "freemium" computer program. That means you can download and use Evernote without paying any money, although you won't be able to access certain features and services. If you want to enjoy all of the benefits offered by this app, you should pay a premium fee.

For many people, Evernote is a great

digital workspace. This cool program allows the user to bookmark webpages and save digital content (e.g. news, emails, and search results). Evernote can help you gather meaningful words and motivational ideas. In addition, it can greatly improve your productivity.

Here are some of the features offered by Evernote:

- It can "read" – Evernote has OCR (i.e. Optical Character Recognition), a functionality that allows it to scan and recognize text. You can use OCR on different sources of information. For example, you can use it to read texts contained in a PDF document, an old photograph, a news article, etc.

If you are in a picture, holding a Gibson guitar, Evernote's OCR capability will scan the "Gibson" brand (and whatever text it sees) and save them into the system. When this happens, the word "Gibson" will become a searchable term for your Evernote account.

- It enhances your "email experience" – If you are using Evernote, the application will provide you with an email address. You may use this email account to save important files (e.g. pictures, documents, messages, newsletters, attachments, etc.) without affecting your personal email account. Alternatively, you may use both email addresses when using the application: the Evernote email account will serve as a backup storage.

- It allows you to access your files easily – Since this application is "cross-platform," you may access the files and documents stored in your gadgets. With Evernote, your files will be synchronized automatically. That means you can retrieve the files stored in your desktop computer using your smartphone.

Many students use Evernote to "carry" their textbooks and study notes. Teachers and professors, on the other hand, use the application to store their lesson plans and exam papers. Career professionals may scan and store important presentations, research papers and trade journals. If you are buying groceries, you may save your shopping list on Evernote and access it using your tablet or smartphone once you are in the supermarket. Evernote allows you to store and/access information easily. You will certainly benefit from it, regardless of your profession or status in life.

- It allows users to create "voice notes" – If you are using a smartphone, you may create voice notes through the Evernote phone application. You just have to say the things you want to take note of, and these will be saved into your account. The information will be synchronized to your other devices such as laptops or tablets. In addition, voice notes are searchable. You can easily access the ones you need.

- It allows you to create a "digital scrapbook" – With Evernote, you can create lots of "notebooks" (maximum is 250) to store the information that matters to you. You can organize the stored information quite easily. You may use tags or divide the data into several categories. If you need to add some info into a notebook, then you just have to access that notebook and drag the file into the notebook area.

- It allows you to save and synchronize website bookmarks – If you are using Evernote, you can simply enter the URL of the webpages that are important to you. These browser bookmarks can be tagged and categorized. It means your browser will be able to work faster. With Evernote, you won't have to access web browsers to save bookmarks.

You can use this application to create those bookmarks and synchronize them across different devices, browsers, and operating systems. To help you remember information about the URLs, you may attach images and notes to each bookmark.

These are some of the powerful features offered by Evernote. As you can see, this application can help you collect and store pieces of information. Wherever you are and whatever you do, Evernote can boost your efficiency and productivity.

Chapter 2: Evernote – Free versus Premium

Evernote can be downloaded and used for free. The decision to upgrade your account depends on the features you need and how you use the service. As of now, Evernote provides its free users with 60 megabytes per month. This capacity is too small for many users, especially for those who love to hoard digital information. These "digital hoarders" prefer to shell out some cash rather than be affected by the 60MB limit imposed by the application developer.

If you are a casual internet user, you may use Evernote as a free user for the rest of your life. For those who are planning to get a premium account, it would be best if you will test the service before paying any money. Use the application for a couple of months and pay attention to the amount of megabytes you consume. If you can survive a month without reaching the limit, then you won't have to spend cash on a premium service that you don't even need.

Here are the benefits enjoyed by premium users:

- The monthly limit is increased – From 60MB, the data limit is raised to 1GB. That means you can save more files and synchronize more information across multiple devices. According to some people, Evernote will be raising these limits soon.

- You may access your files offline –
Free users need to be online in
order to use the application. If you
can't access the internet 24/7, you
may want to upgrade your
account. This will help you ensure
that you can retrieve your files
anytime you need them. If you will
edit your files while you are
offline, the data will be
synchronized as soon as you
connect to the internet again.

- You may share your notebooks –
Premium users may share their
files with others. That means that
other people can view and edit
those documents. This feature is

excellent for work and school projects, online collaboration, family projects, etc.

- You can upload large files – Free users cannot upload a file that is over 25MB. If you are a premium user, this limit is increased to 50MB.

- You may undo changes – Premium users can negate unwanted modifications in their files. They can also retrieve a file that got deleted accidentally. To do this, the user needs to login to their Evernote account, access the History section, and go back to an older version.

- Better security – Premium users

have the option to place a PIN lock on their Evernote account. This feature allows you to secure your files. Other people won't be able to view or edit your files even if they got your devices.

- You may perform PDF searches – All Evernote users can store PDF files in their accounts. However, premium users can perform searches inside those files. This feature is extremely useful if you need to get a piece of information but don't have the time to spend on reading eBooks.

- You may hide the ads – For some people, advertisements are extremely annoying. They can appear at inconvenient times and force you to watch boring content. As a premium user, you may switch those advertisements off.

Chapter 3: The Evernote Desktop Application

According to expert users, Evernote's best feature is its desktop application. New updates and patches are being released regularly, which is the reason why Evernote is a computer program you can always rely on. The desktop application looks great, functions well, and is full of cool features. It allows you to access your files and do whatever you need to do.

After installing the program, you will be required to log in. Evernote will import all of the files in your account as soon as your user credentials are accepted (if you have saved some notes before). Once the information has been synchronized, you will be able to tag, categorize and subcategorize every note. If it's your first time to use Evernote, however, you can just go ahead and create your first content.

The Benefits Offered by the Evernote Desktop Application

- You can take notes even when "offline" – If you have Evernote on your computer, you won't have to use plain note-taking programs like Microsoft's Notepad. You may also create and edit notes even without internet connection. Your notes will be synchronized across all your gadgets as soon as you become online again.

- You won't have to access a web

browser to access your notes – You can simply run the desktop program in order to see your files.

Chapter 4: Evernote – Smartphone Applications

The smartphone versions of Evernote highlight the service's value and usefulness. These applications allow users to create notes, save messages, and access bookmarks whenever they want. Today, Evernote is available for iPhone and Android users. The applications for these two types of phones are almost identical (in terms of design and features). In order to save space, this book will focus on the iPhone version of Evernote.

The iOS Application

The iOS version of Evernote is sleek, simple and beautiful. If you want to create a new note, you just need to tap the blue "+" sign in the middle of the screen. The application allows you to access your tags and notebooks easily. In addition, you may also perform quick searches if you need to get specific pieces of information from your notes. Premium users may add more protection to their files by placing a 4-digit PIN code in their account. Here are some of the features offered by this smartphone application:

- **<u>Evernote Hello</u>** – If you meet many people on a daily basis, you will surely forget some of them. You won't remember their names and where/when you met them. You can solve this problem using Evernote Hello. This feature allows you to save detailed information as soon as you meet the individual.

This can be done in three different ways:

1. You can let the person enter the information – That person may enter his/her name, take a photo (using your phone's camera), and include personal details (e.g. email address, phone number, social media information, etc.).

2. You can enter it for him/her.

3. Get the information from your phone's "Contacts".

- **<u>Create Audio Notes</u>** – Obviously, you will be recording most of your audio notes using a smartphone. This is because you can create those notes comfortably. You may hold the phone as if you are talking to someone. Here are the things you need to do in order to create an audio note:

   1. Press the "+" sign in the middle of the screen.

   2. Write some text to help you identify the recording later on.

   3. Tap the microphone logo (located at screen's top-right corner). This action will start

the recording process.

4. It is time to dictate your note: speak slowly and clearly.

5. Once the note is complete, save it by tapping the "Done" button. The sound file will be stored as an attachment to your note (the text you entered earlier). When you are viewing the note, you will see the size and length of the sound clip. These pieces of information are useful if you are a free user and you want to monitor your data usage. If you don't want to exceed the limits of your free

account, you should always review the size of your audio notes.

You may review the sound file by tapping the arrow key (located in the note's attachment section). Once you are satisfied with the quality of your recording, you can upload it to your Evernote account. You can do this by tapping the "Done" button in the screen's top-left corner. Obviously, you need internet connection in order to upload the file and synchronize it across several devices.

- **<u>Create Webcam Notes</u>** – When people hear about the phrase "webcam note," they often imagine videos recorded for the sole purpose of storing notes. However, this assumption is incorrect. Creating a webcam note means you will take a photo (using a webcam) and upload it to your Evernote account. It's more of a glorified version of "selfies." However, these "simple" pictures can be turned into detailed accounts of your daily life. All you need to do is add some information about things that are important to you. That means an ordinary photo album can serve as an archive of vital info you can review in the future.

- **Evernote Peek** – This

application is available for iPhone and iPad users. Evernote Peek allows you to acquire lots of information through the use of digital flashcards. It works great if you own the iOS smart cover since you can open the flap at the gadget's end to "peek" at the info it provides you.

The Peek feature of Evernote is useful in interacting with the digital notebooks. You may create your own notebooks through your devices or download ones shared by other people.

- **Evernote Food** – This feature lets you to preserve the memory of the great food you eat. With this feature, you can take a photo of your meal, write a caption, describe the food, mention the place where you bought or ate it, etc. These pieces of information will be stored in your Evernote profile. In addition, the details will be saved in the Evernote Food app. That means you can view the delicious and memorable meals you have eaten whenever you want.

Chapter 5: Tips and Tricks

Now that you are familiar with the basics of Evernote, you are ready for the exciting part – learning how to make your life easier by using this app. This chapter will provide you with the hottest tips and tricks from expert Evernote users. Since lots of people are using this service, many tricks and hacks are being discovered on a daily basis. That means the ones included here are but just a miniscule fraction of what you can do with Evernote.

Email Your Notes – Many people are doing this. They like to transfer important details from their email account/s into their Evernote profile. They do this because of several reasons:

Evernote's GUI (Graphical User Interface) is better than those of email providers.

Evernote has a powerful search function.

The service can serve as an online scrapbook. You can create your account based on your needs and preferences.

They want to free up some space in their email accounts. Since emails are mostly used for personal and business purposes, it would be great if it will be kept clutter-free.

Email providers (e.g. Gmail, Yahoo!, AOL, etc.) don't allow their users to view information quickly. Basically, you have to open an email in order to view its content and attachments. This can be time consuming, especially if you are receiving lots of emails. Evernote solves this problem by applying a display system that makes use of thumbnail pictures. These "thumbnails" are shown in nice rows, allowing the user to find what they need without opening anything.

It is easy to forward email content to your Evernote account. You just have to send the emails to your Evernote email address. If you don't know this email address, you just have to access you Evernote account and click on the "Usage" button (it is in the top-right corner of the screen). You will be directed to a page that shows your Evernote email account.

You have the option to get a new email address. In that case, you will have to access your Evernote account and reset the email address assigned to you. This option is important if you think that your account's security has been compromised.

Save Your Tweets – There are times when you would love to save a "tweet" so you can read it again later. If you are using Evernote, you may store interesting tweets quickly and conveniently: archive them and turn them into searchable content. You can do this in two different ways:

Using myEN (www.twitter.com/myen) – myEN is an automated system used in Twitter.

It allows users to send tweets to their Evernote accounts. In order to use it, you just have to "follow" the bot and check the message that will be sent to your account. Read the message and click on the link it contains. The screen will show you some details regarding the access privileges needed by the bot. Agree to everything it says (after reading it, of course). Once this is done, the myEN will let you forward important tweets to your Evernote account.

Using IFTTT (www.ifttt.com) – This is an online service designed to automate the user's internet experience. To use it, you just have to access your IFTTT account and click on the "Create" button found in the homepage. Click on the "This" button and select the Twitter icon. The screen will show you 11 choices (this part aims to help you categorize tweets in your Evernote account). You just have to choose the one that best describes the tweet you are working on.

Add Content from Your Google+ Account – Google+ is one of the hottest social networking sites today. If you are an active Google+ user, you can link it to your Evernote account to facilitate easy data transfer. To accomplish this task, you need to:

Set up a Google+ "circle" that contains one member: your Evernote email address. Name the circle so you can identify it easily. You may use whatever name you want.

Save the Google+ thread and share it

through your "Evernote circle." Afterward, the URL for the Google+ discussion will be sent to your Evernote email address.

At this point, you need to remember two things:

You shouldn't invite Evernote to join Google+. Evernote is an automated system: it is not a human being. It won't join any social networking site.

Put a check on the box that says "Email a person not yet using Google Plus). This will ensure that the email will be delivered to your Evernote email address.

Encrypt Your Files – Evernote offers excellent security features. Now, you can encrypt important notes to protect them from other people. Although it is not advisable to store "extremely confidential" information (e.g. online banking and credit card details) in your Evernote account, you can still benefit from its security features. For example, you may use this functionality to protect your files from a nosy friend who loves to access your computer files. To encrypt your files, you need to:

Access the content you need to encrypt.

Highlight the parts of the note you want to protect.

Click on Format – Encrypt – Selected Text. A dialogue box will appear, asking you to set the password for the encrypted content. Enter your chosen password and hit "OK."

Once done, you can check if the encryption worked. Open the note and view your selected part: it should be concealed under a grey bar that has a lock on it.

If you need more encryption features, you may set up a "Truecrypt" account. This service offers more protection for your files. Once the notes have been processed by Truecrypt, you may upload them to your Evernote account. You just have to remember that Truecrypt is a separate service. You may need to pay additional cash if you want to use it.

Use the Desktop Toolbar to Store Important Notes – This tip is applicable for desktop users. As you use

Evernote service, you will observe that you are accessing certain notes regularly. For example, you have a list of things that you want to buy: you may need to update this list on a regular basis.

If you want to access certain notes quickly and conveniently, you should "pin" your selected notes onto the toolbar of the Evernote desktop application. You can do this by clicking on the important note and dragging it to the app's toolbar. If done correctly, the toolbar will display the title of the note. You will be redirected to the note's content once you click on its title.

If you no longer need to access that note often, you can simply drag it away from the app's toolbar. This action will remove the note from the application's "quick access" section. However, the note in question is still stored in your Evernote account.

Create Notes Using Different Kinds of Media – As an Evernote user, you should know that you can use various types of media to create content. You may use text, images, URLs, sound files, and many more to produce high quality notes. That means you can let your imagination control your note-taking procedures.

Create a Table of Contents – If you need to access lots of notes, placing them on the toolbar won't be a great idea. You may get confused with all those little tabs. It would be better if you will categorize your notes and create a table of contents for them. Afterward, you may drag the table of contents to the application's toolbar. This will allow you to easily access the files you need. Since your notes will be organized, you will be able to work on projects efficiently. To create a table of contents, you should:

Open the note you want to include.

Right-click on the note and select "copy note link" from the dropdown menu. This action will save a link to your computer's clipboard.

Create a note that will be used to contain the table of contents. Type the title of the link you are going to enter. Use a title that will help you to identify the note easily.

Highlight the title and right-click. Select "Hyperlink" then "Add."

You will see a dialogue box that asks for a link. Paste the link (using CTRL + V) into the space provided.

Click "OK." The note will display a clickable link. That link will redirect you to the note it was made from.

Repeat the steps 1-6 until you have links for all the important notes.

Share Files, Notes, and Images – You can use Evernote to gather useful bits of information from online sources (e.g. blogs and news articles). Once you have established a library full of these things, you may want to share them with other people. Evernote can help you disseminate your chosen content easily. You may share them through emails and/or social networking sites. However, only premium users can use this feature (i.e. notebook sharing). To share your notes, you should:

Using emails - Check the top section of the screen and click on the "Share" option. Choose the option that says "Send by Email..." Enter the email address of the recipient/recipients and the subject of the message. Type some information regarding the notes you are sending. It would be great if you will provide some descriptions. Once done, click the "Send" button.

Using Twitter or Facebook – Click

on the "Share" option and choose "Post to Facebook" or "Post to Twitter" (depending on your preferred social networking site). This action will open your device's default browser and access your selected social media platform. The screen will provide you with a dialogue box where you can create a message for the recipient, apply privacy settings, and send the note.

Additional Option: Share notes via URLs – If you want to share notes using instant messaging services, you may copy the note's URL onto the device's clipboard. Afterward, paste the web address into the chat box of your instant messaging application.

Share Completed Notes or

Subscribe to Others – This is probably one of the best benefits offered by a premium Evernote account. Premium users may share their notes with either few individuals or the whole planet. In addition, you may run searches for notebooks shared by other people. You may "subscribe" to the content that interests you. The main advantage offered by this feature is that you may share knowledge with other people quickly and easily.

However, the computer system being used by Evernote doesn't support "shared notebook searches." That means Evernote doesn't have a directory of notebooks shared by its users. According to some people, the company's programmers are still working on this feature.

Evernote users find shared notebooks through the use of search engines like Google. The URLs of shared Evernote notebooks begin with "site: http://www.evernote.com/shard/". You can enter that into your favorite search engine and add some keywords for the topic you are interested in. If you are looking for chess strategies, for example, you may access Google and type the following: "site: http://www.evernote.com/shared/ chess strategies."

Create a To-Do List – Many people like to create to-do lists. For them, the simple act of crossing items off as they get completed is a huge boost in mood and productivity. You can create and use great to-do lists using the Evernote application. To make a to-do list, you should:

Create a new note. Open it and right-click on it.

In the dropdown menu, select "To-Do" then "Insert Checkbox."

You will see a checkbox inside the note.

Click on the space near the checkbox (i.e. to place the cursor on that spot) and type the task you want to include.

Repeat steps 2-4 until you have created checkboxes for all of your tasks.

Once a task is completed, you can put a check on the box assigned to that particular task.

Chapter 6: Evernote Plugins and Add-ons

There are lots of available plugins and add-ons for Evernote. This chapter will discuss some of the most popular ones.

- **The Web Clipper** – This plugin is available for web browsers (i.e. Chrome and Firefox). It allows you to clip certain sections from websites easily. Also, once the content is clipped and added to your Evernote account, Web Clipper allows you to view notes related to the clipped web content.

  This plugin is certainly useful for collecting research materials. However, the structure and appearance of the content may change in the Evernote system. The content's actual look may differ from that of the one saved in Evernote: this is due to the codes used in creating the actual post.

- **The Evernote Clearly** – You can download this extension for Chrome and Firefox web browsers. It allows users to convert webpages into simple text (together with the images and links in the webpage). Basically, this extension helps you to remove CSS and HTML coding from online articles. That means the articles will have a simpler look.

- **The Simultaneous Google**

Search – This plugin allows you to run searches on online sources and your own Evernote account. These searches are done simultaneously; hence, the name. For example, you are looking for chess openings. Once you enter the keywords into the Google search box and press the enter button, Google will check both online resources (e.g. articles, images, videos, etc.) and the content in your Evernote account. That means this plugin can help you check whether or not you already have the info you are looking for. It will help you to save time and energy.

Conclusion

Thank you again for downloading this book!

I hope this book was able to help you to master the basics of Evernote.

The next step is to use this application to collect and organize information from online sources.

Finally, if you enjoyed this book, then I'd like to ask you for a favor, would you be kind enough to leave a review for this book on Amazon? It'd be greatly appreciated!

Thank you and good luck!